Love for an Island

The Collected Poems of Phyllis Shand Allfrey

Edited by Lizabeth Paravisini-Gebert

Papillote Press
London and Roseau, Dominica

First published in Great Britain in 2014

A CIP catalogue record for this book is available from the British Library.

Typeset in Courier and Book Antigua
Printed in India by Imprint Digital
Design by Andy Dark
Cover design by Andy Dark

The publication of this volume was made possible in part by a generous grant from Vassar College's Research Committee

ISBN: 9780957118751

Papillote Press
23 Rozel Road
London SW4 0EY
United Kingdom
and Trafalgar, Dominica
www.papillotepress.co.uk

Contents

ROSE O

APPENDIX

Introduction

Then the rush basket lost its twinkling freight
the infant, torn from her enchanted tree,
landed behind a closed suburban gate
leaving as trace a scrap of poetry.

"Changeling"

When Phyllis Shand Allfrey (1908-1986) — author of the classic West Indian novel *The Orchid House* — began her education in Roseau, Dominica, she was fortunate to have both an aunt eager to school her in the British poetic tradition and the Francophone Caribbean's most admired poet of his generation as a family friend and neighbour.

With her maternal aunt, Margaret Nicholls, in charge of her education, Allfrey immersed herself in *The Oxford Book of English Verse*, which she read repeatedly. She felt a particular affinity for Rupert Brooke; and the graceful lyricism of his First World War sonnets would find an echo in Allfrey's own poems of the Second World War.

Nicholls, moreover, was a close friend of Daniel Thaly (1879-1950), a Roseau doctor, who would be a seminal influence on Allfrey's poetic development. Known then as the "Prince of Poets" of the French Antilles, after the noted success of his 1900 collection *Lucioles et Cantharides*, Thaly published — in French — nine very successful volumes of poetry. In the manner of the Creole Parnassian movement of that time, Thaly sought to produce poetry devoid of social context, precise in form, and meticulous in its descriptions of exotic landscapes. Thaly's poems (most often sonnets) were characterised by evocative images of Dominica and Martinique, haunting visions of Africa, and odes to passionate (albeit unrequited) love. His books, some of them inscribed to Margaret, remained among Allfrey's possessions until her death, and she used one of his stanzas as the epigraph to *The Orchid House*.

Allfrey is a difficult writer to place in the West Indian poetic tradition that emerged in the early decades of the twentieth century. Apart from Thaly, her work is contemporaneous with the Négritude poets Aimé Césaire and Nicolás Guillén, whose political ideals she shared. But as a poet, Allfrey lacked their gift for path-breaking, formal experimentation. Moreover, as a white writer, she remained marginal to their primary concern with African-Caribbean affirmation. This marginalisation from the mainstream of Caribbean poetry would grow more marked as subsequent generations of West Indian writers, such as Kamau Brathwaite and Derek Walcott, focussed their work on race, Creole cultures and the region's connections to Africa as the basis of national identities.

Where, then, do we place Allfrey as a Caribbean poet? This is a question awaiting critical analysis, since, except for a handful of texts reproduced in Second World War anthologies, few have had access to Allfrey's poems since their original publication many decades ago. Although she is invariably described as a poet and novelist, her poetry is essentially unknown. For most readers, this book provides their first opportunity to sample her poetic work, some of it out of print since as early as 1940.

A careful perusal of *Love for an Island* will show that the bulk of her poetry was written between 1935 and 1955 (after which her efforts turned towards prose and politics). There are two principal strains to her poetic work: the London-centred poetry of the Second World War, which focusses increasingly on West Indian soldiers and the fight against colonialism; and her Caribbean-centred poetry, which builds upon Thaly's influence but which, unlike his work, seeks to address the social milieu and voices her anti-colonial, anti-racist convictions.

Allfrey came of age as a poet after she settled in England in the mid-1930s with her husband and two infant children, but elements of her lifelong poetic work had been honed earlier, during the years she spent in the United States, living first in New York City and (after her marriage to Robert Allfrey in 1930) in Buffalo, New York. Her earliest surviving poem, "Transfiguration" (1932), which describes the snowy landscape of Buffalo, reflects Allfrey's immersion in a specific subset of New York's literary circles in its experimentation with form, in its urban sensibility and wistfulness.

While in New York City, the young would-be poet had been befriended by Harold Trowbridge Pulsifer, editor of *Outlook Magazine* and a well-known poet who had also been instrumental in fostering the writing careers of two other women poets, Elinor Wylie and Edna St Vincent Millay. Allfrey was working for Pulsifer's mother-in-law as a nanny, and her position in the household brought her into contact with Pulsifer's circle of young American poets, who were striving to adapt traditional poetic forms to modernist approaches and subject matters. The effort to wed traditional forms with a modernism expressed through post-colonial sensitivities and a proto-feminist approach to domestic themes would be the mark of Allfrey's own work. Pulsifer encouraged her to work on her writing — both in verse and prose — and guided her early literary development, continuing to offer advice through the publication of Allfrey's first two collections of poems, until his death in 1948.

In London, Allfrey once again chanced to find employment that gave her access to the city's most prominent poets. Her job as personal secretary to the leftist aristocratic writer Naomi Mitchison placed her on the margins of another literary orbit. Through Mitchison she would meet WH Auden, whose short poems she sought to emulate, Stephen Spender and Stevie Smith. Her admiration for their work, and traces of their influence on her own poetry and prose, are evident in the texts she wrote in the late 1930s. Mitchison's essays on political morality and class conflict also had a profound influence on Allfrey's growing political consciousness and on her poetic subjects.

Nourished by the vibrant literary circle in which she found herself — and having established a friendship with fellow Dominican writer Jean Rhys in London — Allfrey embarked on the writing of her first collection of poetry, *In Circles*, published in 1940 by the Raven Press, a respected small publisher specialising in poetry and drama.

The poems in *In Circles* are thematically and technically very varied; neither *In Circles* (nor any of her subsequent volumes) would develop organically out of a central theme. The collection includes her two best known and most often reprinted "war" poems, "Young Lady Dancing with Soldier" — written for her sister Rosalind, then living with the Allfreys in London — and "Cunard Liner 1940", which was most probably written onboard the ship taking Allfrey back to England after leaving her children with the Pulsifers in the safety of Maine. They evidence the fusion of the personal, the political, and the nostalgia for the fleeting and the losses brought by war that characterises her best poetry.

In Circles displays Allfrey's talent for the evocation of

geography and place. They bring to vivid poetic life a range of spaces she had come to know well: the snowy Maine landscape, the domestic realm of unfulfilled female lives, the "saddest mood" of a beleaguered London during the Blitz. This evocation is achieved through her keen eye for detail, not only of the smells, sounds and textures but also the class distinctions, the small cruelties, the loneliness and ephemeral contacts.

Three poems in the collection address Allfrey's West Indian heritage. In "The White Lady", inspired by the statue of the Empress Josephine standing in a circle of palms in a public square in Fort-de-France, Martinique, Allfrey assumes the collective voice of black West Indian women to address the class and race differences sustained in the name of empire; differences that have always separated women in the Caribbean. It is her first attempt at writing from the perspective of black women – her second will be that of Lally, the narrator of *The Orchid House*. In "To Roma (Luxembourg Gardens)", written to Thaly's adopted daughter (Allfrey's maternal cousin and the model for the character of Coralie in *The Orchid House*), she seeks to bridge the gulf between white and coloured women through its homage to the beauty of the coloured girl. It also plays tribute to Thaly, who in "Au Jardin du Luxembourg" (from *Nostalgies Françaises*, 1913) finds in the vigorous swaying branches of its copses the haunting aura of his tropical isle. "These People are Too Stolid" is Allfrey's first attempt to address the withering away of those "fed on hurricanes, songs by moonlight, pomalaks" when they are away from their native soil. She will return to this theme in the "Stella" section of *The Orchid House*, where her character contrasts the beautiful but sterile landscape of Maine with the teeming, sustaining, green world of her island.

Although there were no reviews in the press, the collection came to the attention of Mitchison's literary circle, especially that of the Labour politician Aneurin Bevan, who in 1941 had become editor of *Tribune*, a weekly founded by the Labour Left. Under Bevan's leadership, *Tribune* began publishing Allfrey's poems, short stories and book reviews.[1] Sharing the newspaper's pages with such as Stevie Smith and George Orwell, Allfrey published poems like "Colonial Soldiers" about the West Indian servicemen "who were born and breathed in open spaces" and "Colonial Committee" where she writes, in frustration, of the early days of the decolonisation process (a result of her work with the Committee on West Indian Affairs).

Her poems in *Tribune* form the core of her second volume of poetry, *Palm and Oak*, published in 1950. The title, she wrote, was meant to invoke "the tropical and Nordic strains" in her ancestry. The collection addresses her experiences with helping West Indian migrants settle into London in "Expatriates". Here she asks how "the exiles from enchanted isles/tend and sustain their rich nostalgic blaze", expressing the vital link between exile and her homeland. This will be echoed some years later in what is perhaps her most quoted poem, "Love for an Island". The wilting of the West Indian in England is again described, this time in "Changeling".

The collection boosted Allfrey's growing reputation as a writer. One of its poems, "While the Young Sleep", won a poetry competition judged by Vita Sackville-West, thus bringing her work to the greater attention of writers and critics. The encouragement and inquiry as to whether she had ever written a novel led to *The Orchid House*, a manuscript quickly accepted for publication by Constable and published in 1953 to enthusiastic reviews.

Palm and Oak is perhaps the most deeply political of her four poetic volumes. It is also, however, the most deeply meta-literary, the one in which she addresses most directly the nature and tribulations of her choice of a writing life. "Poet's Cottage", for example, a description of a visit to Dove Cottage, where William Wordsworth had lived for several years, contrasts Wordsworth's writing ("heedless of clamour and cooking smells...having claimed the daffodil and daisy as his own") to the tormented writing life of the cottage's other famous tenant, Thomas De Quincey, who "craved the bright and healthy, but...saw/flowers as weeds and weeds as opiates". "Changeling" speaks of the child that leaves behind her "a scrap of poetry" after being "translated/into a strange and unfamiliar grove". "Tapestry" speaks to the transformative power of creativity and of the "silver needle [that] binds and plies/past into waking dream, time to touch,/touch into web of sweetest agonies,/*dream into real, life into tapestry.*"

In 1954 Allfrey returned to Dominica (where her husband had been hired by L Rose & Company) and was actively involved in the founding of the Dominica Labour Party and its first political campaign. It was a period when her growing political commitment to furthering the interests of the estate workers had led to her husband's dismissal from his job and her virtual ostracism from Dominican society.

Then, in 1955, in Dominica, she published a third collection,

Contrasts. And, as with her earlier collections, the reader can trace the developments of themes closely tied to her geographical circumstances. Relying heavily on melodious language, rhyming schemes, and elegiac tones, the poems of *Contrasts* — her most lyrical collection — are also Allfrey's most personal and intimate, and are particularly rich in their evocation of domestic spaces and Dominica's tropical landscapes. Hence the poignancy of her declaring her "love for an island" as "the sternest passion", hence the haunting and vivid recreation of the "warm white pallor of a tropic night" in the charming "Nocturne" and the "citrus dark" of "Fugitive Hummingbird".

Contrasts is also the most "tropical" of Allfrey's collection. In poems like "Nocturne" and "The Nights" we can see her poetic voice draw upon traditional rhythmic and metric patterns to impart on the texts a musical lyricism consistent with the models she imbued from her readings of Daniel Thaly and other Creole Parnassians. The traditional metre and rhyme scheme of "Love for an Island", Allfrey's signature poem, for example, is both anachronistic and, as such, most effective. It gives the poem an artless musicality that serves as the ideal vehicle for the sentimental nature of its celebration of the poet's love for her home island as "the sternest passion:/ pulsing beyond the blood through roots and loam."

The mid-1950s were also years in which Allfrey became a committed Federalist and sacrificed her literary career to her political aspirations. In the short-lived West Indies Federation she was elected as one of the two Dominican representatives to the Federal Parliament, and became Minister of Social and

Labour Affairs, the only woman and the only white person in the Cabinet. After the collapse of the Federation and a controversial expulsion from the political party she had founded, in 1965 Allfrey and her husband began publication of an opposition paper, *The Star*, which cultivated and encouraged local writers. *The Star* was to become the government's severest critic, and Allfrey created a poetic persona, Rose O, through which she would echo the people's anger at the government. As Rose O, Allfrey published clever satires often using the local vernacular or French Creole.

Allfrey's involvement in the Federation and her subsequent career as a newspaper editor led to an 18-year gap between the publication of *Contrasts* and that of her next collection, *Palm and Oak II*, published in 1973. The volume included a number of poems from previous collections, some poems published more than two decades before in British journals and newspapers and not previously collected, and a handful of new poems, notably "Trio by Lamplight", written for her son David, one of two Kalinago boys she had adopted in the early 1960s, and "The Child's Return", dedicated to Jean Rhys (to whom she assiduously sent *The Star*). The poems published earlier included "Lone Cactus", a tender attempt to explain her husband's characteristic aloofness, and "Beethoven in the Highlands", inspired by her playing a recording of Beethoven's Fifth Symphony during a wartime visit to Naomi Mitchison in Scotland. The collection's most notable thematic departure is that of "Ghosts in a Plantation House", Allfrey's only poem alluding to the legacy of the plantation in Dominica, and an echo of Allfrey's anti-colonial novel *The Orchid House*.

In the late 1970s, in an effort to re-establish her literary career, Allfrey resumed work on an autobiographical novel she had begun in 1962, *In the Cabinet*, but it remained unfinished at her death in 1986. By then her literary - although not her political - legacy had been mostly forgotten by her fellow Dominicans. She lived long enough to see *The Orchid House* republished (in 1982, Virago) but there were no more poems. More recently, with the publication of her short stories, *It Falls Into Place* (2004, Papillote Press) and in the tributes paid to her and her work at Dominica's annual literary festival, we are at last seeing a reclaiming of her literary reputation. Together with a renewed academic interest in her writing, she is being rightly placed as a Dominican, and more broadly, a Caribbean writer. A position which would surely have given her great pleasure.

---

1. Throughout the 1940s and early 1950s, Allfrey had also turned her attention to prose, writing and publishing a number of short stories in *Tribune* and *The Manchester Guardian*. Most of these stories are collected in *It Falls Into Place* (Papillote Press, 2004).

In
Circles

1940

Sitting around in circles, the prudent people
Eat the mystical hot flesh of the brave and bold.
How adequate to devour the lives of others!
How just to grow fat, respectable and old.

To Phina and Philip

THE GIPSY TO HER BABY

For Phina

Oh flower of my flesh, whose blossoming
Brought me wild pain and even wilder joy,
Immortally delightful baby thing,
Less than an angel, greater than a toy:
Out of my body's darkness rudely torn
To navigate the ocean of the world
That men might boast — *another babe is born,*
Another flag of challenge is unfurled!

How you will roam, and whither, who can guess?
All that I give you is a heritage
Of bold adventuring and loveliness,
Of merriment, and wisdom amply sage;
Take these few weapons in your tiny hands
And sally forth to meet a crouching fate.
Bless with your darling presence many lands:
Bless with your love your heart's true intimate.

THE WHITE LADY
Martinique

The white ladies walk between the trees,
choosing their steps with care, so as not to soil
their shoes, which are whiter than their faces:
for these are the untarnished ones, the wives of
    officials.
We are the trees, we are the silent spies,
we know their gowns are imported from Paris,
and therefore precious,
we know that they conceive their children in rooms
with the jalousie blinds drawn, the mosquito net
    tucked in.
We are not jealous of that love-making:
happy we are to dig our roots firm into the earth,
happy we are to be brown and strong and lissome.
Our children are multiple, and all have beauty:
we fear not dirt, nor age. There was but one we
    feared,
and she was a queen:
she wore an old purple dress and the bees settled
    on it,
and her dark nurse prophesied darkly of power —
of love and wars, desertion and death;
and the poets turned their eyes away from us,
to write poems about her: sweet lewd poems,
for she was light and sweet and proud to love.
They called her Marie-Josèphe-Rose
Taschez de la Pagerie de Beauharnais,
saying the words like music;
but he called her Joséphine, and Phina in the
    dark of the night.
Now are the bees flown,

now is our fear flown,
now we have no rival:
she stands among the palms,
among the royal palms,
whiter than the wives of officials
and whiter than Caribbean surf,
as white as marble, with her face lifted to the
    wind,
listening for the word Phina
in the deep of the night,
and the tourists say
her gown is Empire.

FLYING POINT

Such a small road, and yet so dangerous;
So full of traps and pitfalls, bright with glare
Of winter ice; but suddenly for us
The low white house, a Trappist hostel, looms
And the immense black shape of dog or bear
Trundles us up the slope to lighted rooms.

Everything hangs so sweetly on the walls,
And words hang ardently and insecure
On visiting lips and hosts': a silence falls
While lines are cast for speech that will endure.
Ah, comrades! In your bay the enduring sea,
The frozen sea which has no social grace,
Remains completely still, in mockery
Of this one's posture and of that one's face.

Inside, a fire crackles and the sparks fly,
Fine food and drink make minds and bodies hot:
Snow-white and Rose-red jest: impulses die,
But much that is unsaid rests unforgot.

DECAYED GENTLEWOMAN

Oh sad winter of the heart,
Oh stripped leaves of the soul
Falling upon the barren part,
Falling upon the barren whole

Oh cold buds of lips unkissed
Frozen on the bending branch,
Oh twigs of hope that untwist
Blackened by an avalanche

Oh sad winter, drain the clot
Of sap from the decaying tree,
Fell it straight and let it rot
For other lives' fertility.

ONE FINE DAY

Most usually, one sees
the Bishop's trees
from our bedroom window;
but today it was quite extraordinary:
hearing a shout
and looking out,
whom did we observe
to swerve
in airy funicular curve,
but Hans and Thea,
old Frau Tiefenbrunn,
Burghard Taubeles,
and sweet little Liesel Petermeier.
They landed on the lawn
and in the allotments
to the accompaniment of machine-gun fire
shortly after dawn.

Thea really resembled
a double parachute,
for her skirts flew up in the breeze
revealing her bloomers,
but Hans was hardly dissembled:
he wore his pin-striped suit
Made in England, if you please.
Burghard Taubeles, after stooping
to pick some spinach, retired pooping
at our neighbours in the lower flats.
Alas! the poor head porter got riddled
while our local Wardens fiddled
with their air-guns, masks, buckets of sand and

        tin hats.
Frau Tiefenbrunn unfolded her bicycle
and rode it smartly
though the Vicar's gate.
She looked so energetic and *Kraft durch Freude*,
we quite forgot, until it was too late,
that she had died of a goitre
in 1938.
Thea moved into the air-raid shelter,
but she soon moved out again
because there were no windows to clean;
as she emerged, it began to rain,
helter-skelter —
the way it rains in England.
So up they came in the lift
(Liesel, Thea and Hans)
fresh from a visit to France.
And had they come to repay
the £3 10 they borrowed
On Coronation Day?
Far from it: they had come to stay.
"Take off my boots," Hans cried.
"Coffee for all, beside."
But in spite of our national pride
it was an unusual party,
quite hearty
in the good *Norddeutscher* way.
How sweet the memories! *Erinnerst du dich an…?*
The Russian cigarettes Hans parcelled out
wrapped us in aromatic smoke.
We folk
forgot the implication stern and solemn
that we might seem like members

of the Fifth Column;
there was so very much to talk about.
Oh fatal memories! We hurt our guests
without intention
by a reminder, a remark
that was a little bit too stark:
we spoke of things good fascists would not mention.
Liesel apologised
before she shot,
but that was not
much compensation.
It is hard to forgive
with a brain like a sieve!

Adequately disguised
in our best clothes
the visitors rose
and made their way coolly to the railway station.

YOUNG LADY DANCING WITH SOLDIER

Young lady dancing with soldier,
Feeling stern peaty cloth with your slight hand,
So very happy,
So happy
To be dancing with the patriotic male —
You have forgotten
deliberately
(Or perhaps you were never concerned to know)
Last month your partner was a shipping clerk.

How, as he sat by his few inches of window,
This boy dreamed of ships and far engagements,
Battles with purpose
and future,
Fair women without guile, and England's honour,
Comme chevalier
sans peur...
But instead he got conscripted into the Army,
And now you are the last symbol of his dream.

It is rather thrilling to be a last symbol,
Before mud clogs the ears, blood frets the mouth
Of the poor clerk
turned soldier,
Whose highest fortune will be to find himself
Conscripted back
to life...
Done up like a battered brown paper parcel —
No gentleman, *malgré tout*; clerk unemployed.

HOUSE OF TODAY

And if I call your house
The house of today,
Will the walls make answer?
Sweet walls, brown and gay,
Spattered with stars and dressed
By deft male hands but by a woman's choice.
If you could speak, what would you say?
What would you say, if you had a voice?

   ...Oh we are old, too old
   To look behind or before,
   We ask that they be kind
   And cherish us: no more.
   We ask for low voices,
   Laughter, the lovers' duel,
   Safety, good paint,
   And the right kind of fuel.

Ah, but house —
Standing secure and still,
Snug and escapist in
The little curve of the hill —
That is the life of wood,
Of wood and stone,
But not the ardent life
Of blood and bone.
Already the little mice
Carve a future out of the floor,
A cat streaks panther-trails on the roof
And a child waits cold at the door.

MAINE

In Maine the air is crystal — winter lies
White ermine on brown velvet, and the frost
Drips from bare twigs like jewels of delight.
Tender free landscape, for a little space
So much my home, so true my goal and refuge —
Goodbye: let tears of snow muffle my grief.
Out into darkness, out into sorrow sailing
Away from sunshine and the small-town lights,
Voices of children, grave New England songs,
Corn-muffins, lobster, Californian wine,
Flavour of love and hospitality...
Goodbye: I guard you as a winter's tale,
A taste in the mouth, the sturdy grasp of friends,
Golden-lit windows, the sensation of living.
Goodbye: let tears of snow muffle my grief.

CUNARD LINER 1940

Now, for the last time, total solitude.
The ship hangs between explosion and quiet
    forward driving,
The faces of the passengers are grave.
Oh what is this sobriety which so denudes us
Of the sarcastic cough, the cackling laughter,
The thin flirtation and the importance of black
    coffee after?
Of course, we are all being British, all being
    ourselves,
All knowing we carry Empire on our shoulders:
But even so, we are exceptionally grave.
Voices: "My husband's heavily insured."
"I said to stewardess, get baby into the boat!"
"I carry pneumonia tablets in my old army bag."

Yes, friends, but if we had no time to scramble
For babies, tablets and insurance papers,
What would the U-boat's dart, the spurting mine
Mean to each one of us? The end of *what*?

The end of helpless dignity for the army officer!
The end of dancing for the golden girl:
The end of suckling babies for the mother:
The end of study for the gangling youth:
The end of profit for the business men:
The end of brave sea-faring for the crew:
But for so many it would be the end of nothing,
Of nothing nicely done and dearly cherished.

And for myself? oh darling, for myself

It would be life's most true and fatal end;
It would be the conclusion in my brain
And my most spirited heart and my fair body
Of you — the last rich consciousness of you.

TO LONDON

Beleaguered city, humming under the moon,
Constant in form, fickle in sound and tone,
Fold your grey arms about me, for I swoon —
Sick with all wars. City, your evening moan
Is for lost soldiers, and the ragged young
Who wander without learning, without food
In the grim streets and alleys cobweb-flung.
City, of what avail your saddest mood
When there are those who still can float the air
With mirth that springs from military joys,
From Pyrrhic gains, the wasted young and fair,
The Service women and the khaki boys?
Oh drop a thousand veils over the brass
Of bugles, buttons and the glib appeal
Of all that shines to make a war surpass
The ordinary decencies men feel.

THESE PEOPLE ARE TOO STOLID

These people are too stolid
for my frail self.
Insubstantial I watch them,
like a waiter at the Ritz,
like a skeleton waiter
padded with the defence
of a different way of life —
a birth between the palms
of a Caribbean mound.
There is a difference
in the diet of spirits,
for some are fed on hurricanes,
songs by moonlight, pomalaks,
coconut milk, yams and the
mysterious granadilla.
Others feed on wood and iron,
they grow stolid
on a diet of plumbing,
books, chairs, lamb cutlets,
houses and hard facts;
there is always a war on
between the stolid spirits and the frail,
and the stolid spirits always win:
but the frail spirits have a final strategy
— they vanish.

TO ROMA
Luxembourg Gardens

We have inherited this lovely place
Just for an hour. It was the haunt of kings;
But, Roma, when I look into your face
I think of other proletarian things.

I think how beauty knows no frontier bar
Even when all the world is going mad:
Child of mixed blood, how exquisite you are!
Despite the circling frenzy, I am glad.

Paris sees just a blonde and a brunette
Strolling between the flower beds. But I
See something else which I shall not forget.
And so, adieu; auf Wiedersehen; good-bye.

SALUTE

Meeting me in the road, he greets me: comrade.
Rough music in that word, rude magic
In grip of clenching fist on willing hand.
This is our barricade against the tragic
Creeping decomposition of our land.
Comrade, he says: and by my oath, he says
Just what he means. We can break bread, blend tears,
Share work and conflict, go our different ways
Supported through our afternoons and years
By certain concord sprayed a thousandfold
Like springtime in the country of the mind.
We shall grow old
And separate, but find
Always in roads and lanes and streets and squares
Echoes of old salutes, rough music and rude magic —
Comrades.

Palm
and
Oak

1950

EXPATRIATES
West Indians in Britain*

Living in sunless reaches under rain,
how do the exiles from enchanted isles
tend and sustain their rich nostalgic blaze?

Those who are crazed and lone ignite in pain,
but some stoke inner fires with golden wiles
and some feed sparsely on rare lambent days.

Others grow charred to ash on memories;
and one estranged beats poems thin as leaves
out of stored tropic heat on brumal nights

of fearful mist and chill. Another his
whole radiance concentrates, loves more than
    grieves:
sparks from his heart and lips betake their
    flights.

---

* Originally published as "Exiles," Allfrey changed the title and added the subtitle when the
poem was reprinted in *Palm and Oak II*.

POET'S COTTAGE

An owl's half-sister turns the creaking key,
opens the door and leads her clients in.
Clutching their tickets and old memories
of classroom recitations, they advance —
eyes all apop for the domestic scene:
at last they merge the poet in the man.
Portraits of relatives and local views
are soon dismissed — but here's the pint-sized jug
from which the poet's sister sprinkled drops
of dewy lakeland water on her kind
and intellectual face: the red-hung bed
where children were begotten cozily
while the huge mind embraced another love.
And here friends visited; and here he wrote,
heedless of clamour and of cooking smells
from the dim dungeon kitchen; this is where
the spicy garden bursts into the house
at unexpected level. Here he built
steps to a tiny knoll; these roots he laid.

But who of all the guests still lingers here,
bitterly envious of domestic bliss?
'Tis the inheritor of all but peace,
that restless tenant who for twenty-six
hungry and bitter years lived in the shade
of his anxiety and helpless grief.
He craved the bright and healthy, but he saw
flowers as weeds and weeds as opiates;
and not a nurse majestic and divine.
Reaching for light, he touched the shadowed walls
and soon became their shadow, while his great

and unbegirt forerunner had escaped
into the yellow sunshine, having claimed
the daffodil and daisy as his own.

BEFORE A TAPESTRY

So rich at last her tapestry of dream
the brown silk hound between the *fleur-de-lys*
leaps the confining stitches of its frame
baying against his absence in the flesh.
Two swans clip in a blush of sunset light;
the terrace to the keep shows mossy prints
where to his wimpled beauty runs the knight;
O troubadour, sewn tight to her heart's mesh!
Young heralds knee-deep in mosaic buds
chant tender roundelays and palinodes:
the grass-bound peacock flaunts his jewelled studs.
Turret-locked captive, love makes near and free!
Desire's silver needle binds and plies
past into waking dream, time into touch,
touch into web of sweetest agonies,
dream into real, life into tapestry.

NOW IN OUR TIMES

Now our times' constriction, who will beat
brain against cell,
and who will lift head to find there is no ceiling?
Beyond the body-confining prison, boundless swell
of thought outpouring to unfenced terrain
where each inhabits his private heaven or hell.

Now in our times' frugality, who will stand
patient in dragnet crowd
to purchase measured bounty, and who will break
an easy-gotten loaf between his proud
and simple friends? Oh who will value more
even than bread the life to him allowed?

Now in our times' confusion, who can see
the relativity
of freedom, which means various things to men,
and plenty, which is dark satiety
to one, and to another the sufficient?
Oh who knows sure when he is full and free?

The grain lies warm upon a painted landscape.
Clear eyes can feed
like birds on yellow; the heart aware bounds swift
from its strict limitations and is freed,
leaving the cage to the statebound and frustrated
and the slaves of greed.

WHILE THE YOUNG SLEEP

Turbulent striplings, now that you are couched
straight in your narrow beds, your fair limbs flexed,
now — while the wind howls and the sleet-rain drips —
scattered are textbooks over which you slouched,
dispersed the heartless words that briefly vexed
maternal ears; dreaming the youth-soft lips.

Calmly at ease the solitary, kneeling
to take your tangled debris in her hands,
turns from the window with its threat of storm...
Withdrawing into herself at last in feeling
she has escaped from heights of your demands
into a vale where it is still and warm.

Marvellous freedom of a lonely room,
treasures at handsreach dormant, all the past
in the slow downsweep of a silver brush
through burnished hair... banished the lively fume
of growth and challenge, now at his languid last
comes self-remembrance in delicious hush.

Sleep, younglings, sleep.
She dreams; you lie quite still,
but she is quick with liberated thought
and over all the night broods like a dove.
Spent is the effort of the straining will;
a yielding softness reigns; shy bliss is caught
and rests in fancy in the arms of love.

THE TRUE-BORN VILLAGER
*(For West Indian Migrants in Britain)**

The true-born villager will thatch a village
deep in metropolis. He draws a line
round the arena of his daily trudging
and shocks pedestrians with bright good-morrows;
shrewd as a fieldmouse, weaves his one-track way
through the great wheatfields of the rustling crowds
    with a whoa, whoa, the grey sheep-backs,
    the woollen coats of shoppers.

He gleans the primrose faces of the young,
paled by unnatural lighting, reading them
simply as other men absorb the news:
and when the headlines scream at him of China
he knows that China's smaller than his village.
Oh there's a man has alchemy to turn
flats into cottages! What's love to him?
A long and stoical mating. And what's death?
The hewing of a tree that's served its term:
    logs for the living.

* Subtitle added when reprinted in *Palm and Oak II.*

THE PERFECTION SEEKERS

With what resentful hearts
do the perfection seekers
arrive at boundaries
of their idyllic hopes!

There are those who love
like harsh and wonderful bigots,
brooking no heresy.
Once let the shadow
the sullying spot
the imprint of doubting
fall on their idol,
all good is forgot.

Torn from the monolith
granite of memory
all the frail ivy-green
tendrils of pleasure.
All the fair kindness,
the laughter, the feasting,
the miracle-sharing
was never, was not
all good is forgot.

With what embittered hearts
do the perfection seekers
arrive at monuments
to their idyllic hopes!

COLONIAL COMMITTEE*

The plushy jungle of the ancient room
parts to admit the hunted and the hunter
who drawn by stress of century and war
greet as old friends with ripe commercial banter;

lianas of good will hang from the ceiling,
and down those strands the little restless apes
of compromise and cavil swing and jabber,
like dots upon the Empire's ticker-tapes.

Framed on a northern wall, the oily eye
Of noble Lord looks trustee-wise upon
The olive and mahogany and white
Of the assembled faces, but no frown

hints at the terminating trusteeship,
or at the adolescence too prolonged;
for in this civil jungle scarce a snarl
or yap of pain attests the deeply wronged.

Yet certain members see the phosphorous trail,
the orchids hung with scorpions, the agouti
which mocking from its palm-top, gibbers loud
that there are things more urgent than cold duty,

and certain members hear the rush of rains
in hot impatient lands, and feel the flood
surging to make the plushy wilderness
a monsoon island in a sea of blood.

* This poem was first published in *Tribune* before the liberation of India. (Allfrey's note)

CHANGELING

The child was not bewitched, but was translated
into a strange and unfamiliar grove
wherein that helpless infant, sad created,
fell soft beneath the downy spell of love.
She borrowed from her watchers certain looks
and mimicked their hereditary ways;
she slept beside a cataract of books:
words charged her inarticulate first days.
Even her little times of grief and glee
swift matched the moods of her attendant sprite;
her flesh attained the bloom of fantasy,
her eyes attained the blue stars of delight.
Yet always lurked the fear that in a snatch
the changeling child would vanish as she came;
within that secret grove her friends could catch
the trivial echoes of an earthbound name.
Then the rush basket lost its twinkling freight
the infant, torn from her enchanted tree,
landed behind a closed suburban gate
leaving as trace a scrap of poetry.

THE IVORY ROSE

Instant the flicker of love by a look by a touch
becomes substantiate, becomes an ivory rose
chiselled to wear at the breast, in scented hair
cold, but rooted in life: silent swan effigy
on black silk lake: frozen in tinsel hay
as tangled butterflies to wax transfigured.

Rose of ivory
sculptured to bear perpetual testament
to pink spread petals caught in opal glare
of a white doorway: moment of goodbye
fresh as the splash of water, faint as blush.

Rose of ivory
crushed and distilled from crimson rage and tears
on wine-soaked velvet to etiolate
cream rose of courage without hope, the pale
crimped ear which listens for the never-nearing step

Sharp, sharp the ivory petals, keen as glass,
and permanent the nimbus at the heart
which gives no heat and presages no grief
being carved beauty, calm and moony still,
fractured by ripples like a star in mud
over which human shadows cross and waver.

WIND FROM THE PARK

The lost friend, being humbler than the lost
    love, and more sane,
falls from life's pressings book like a dried herb,
    leaving no stain.

The dried herb drifts away, but the crushed rose
    cleaves and grows dark
and drops in an empty hand when there blows
    wind from the park.

RESISTANCE*

And this: the living outside ourselves: the wrench
dragging our deep and comfortable roots
out of earth sockets, out of the sweet of home
into what wilderness and icy air
of other men's danger, terror and defeat?
See us, stretched human-gentle by the window,
suddenly stung by a word, a Postman's knock,
a chord of music into remembered action.
Watch us unwilling stir, read the grooved frown
which speaks divided loyalty, and see
how sad we lay our book, our sleeping child,
our need for symphony and safety by,
stiff rising like the wounded, straight to open
the door which leads to a dark and troubled wood —
knowing ourselves half lost before we find it!
Against our cheeks the tendrils of reproach
whip in the storm; the leaves of the book blow wild
for their lost reader; the infant screams, abandoned
the symphony fades, the safe walls hug no tenant.
Reproach without reward — that is our choice;
for in a world well stacked with organised armies
we, spurning armchair trenches, join the Guerrillas
and plunge in the dark to seek that pilgrim band
whose faces we shall always recognise.

* Originally untitled, this title was added when the poem was reprinted in *Palm and Oak II*.

42

Contrasts

1955

NOCTURNE

O warm white pallor of a tropic night!
Firm stand the hills, washed by a crystal moon
which hovers like some perfume-laden kite
or drips and sways, a carnival balloon.
The milky clouds unfold their snowdust pile;
fair stand the hills; the moon floats low, and drips
intoxicating silver on an isle
of dark seduction. Round her sable hips
the sea, a pleated sparkling petticoat,
unfurls to girdle closer. In a white
delirium we humans drift afloat
within the pallor of a tropic night,
our mortal shadows gliding brown as bark
spangled with nutmeg, cinnamon and lime;
rich songs assail the hidden glades of dark
beyond the laundered landscape of delight.
O warm white pallor of a tropic night!

THE HIDDEN HAMLET
near Battle, England

There is a house that does not wish to be found.
Small stars like centaury and pimpernel
creep to its walls, which crouch into the ground
that dwarfish trees may hide them, and a swell
of meadow terrace fretted with green spray
gently conceals them from the groping sight.
I have known men go mad on a clear day,
tortured in thickets, having wandered right
up to its lintel — smothered in a pall
of wild white roses at the very end.
I have known strangers hunt for it, but all
calling for guidance to some unseen friend.
Perhaps the poor sad ghost whose nightdress blazed
once when the hamlet teemed with working life,
cast her soft spell upon it, so that dazed
by its unlooked-for leisure, rarely sought
save by the accidental questing eye,
the hamlet shrinks from the aggressive joys
of her too live successors, and is shy
of the loud earthly steps of girls and boys.

THE NIGHTS

The short days of light make the long nights of love
Relinquish, relinquish a tissue of sun
for infrangible velvet of ebon and mauve
Oh my ormolu darling, my opaline one.

The long days of light make the short nights of sleep
now the hyacinth shadows are flaxen and bright
and the threne turns gambado; the gridelin steep
of the stairs in the dream are foreshortened by light

Keep the long days for living, the long nights for us
when your grey eyes are aloes and monticoline
move the ebony shapes on a cloud fabulous,
Oh my ormolu darling, crepuscular queen.

LOVE FOR AN ISLAND

Love for an island is the sternest passion:
pulsing beyond the blood through roots and loam
it overflows the boundary of bedrooms
and courses past the fragile walls of home.

Those nourished on the sap and milk of beauty
(born in its landsight) trembled like a tree
at the first footfall of the dread usurper —
a carpet-bagging mediocrity.

Theirs is no mild attachment, but rapacious
craving for a possession rude and whole;
lovers of islands drive their stake, prospecting
to run the flag of ego up the pole,

sink on the tented ground, hot under azure,
plunge in the heat of earth, and smell the stars
of the incredible vales. At night, triumphant,
they lift their eyes to Venus and to Mars.

Their passion drives them to perpetuation:
they dig, they plant, they build and they aspire
to the eternal landmark; when they die
the forest covers up their set desire.

Salesmen and termites occupy their dwellings,
their legendary politics decay.
Yet they achieve an ultimate memorial:
they blend their flesh with the beloved clay.

TURN THE LEAVES

Turn the leaves of my heart's book:
mark with your silver pen the shaming phrases;
disrobe the family portraits, and espy
the clues, the passwords to maturity, the gay
infatuations, petrifying fears.
Turn, turn the pages, note the changing script —
ragged to round and round to elegant,
elegant to impatient, and impatient
to inconsistent sensitivity. Now score
the underlying question on each sheet
and draw a line between the plaited past
and the untangling present. Here, my love,
the writing becomes your own; consonant "I"
stands like a birch tree in a bright new land;
ciphers are servants to our fealty;
nothing's significant to be recorded
beside the outflowing journal of allegiance —
chronicle of a concord strange and deep.
Obliterate the question-mark, add stars
for commas, and forbid forever
the full-stop as a sign we refuse to know.

WITH TIME A THREATENED CURRENCY

With time a threatened currency, when once
a beatific interval is given
wise fools indulge themselves as in a trance,
jealous lest any dividend be riven.

The air embalmed within unceilinged walls
drenched with a garden fragrance, comes to be
another element than air: footfalls
thunder in vaults; knocks rend felicity.

With time a threatened currency, and space
an indefensive citadel, enough
ransom is paid for the beloved face
to jeopardise the solvency of love.

FUGITIVE HUMMINGBIRD

No bird stirs in the aromatic dark
        no bird sings
and night wheels hotly on unfeathered wings,
        with scrape and cark
        of crickets, frogs,
        famished pariah dogs
and all the other restless brindled things.

Those pricks of stars which dive and cling to bark
        like lamps aprowl
seek lost birds, light only on an owl
        which has been stark
        reduced to bones
        round coalpot stones;
never did hunger pay so dear for fowl.

   In the accordion-pleated palms
   doves lately moaned for alms…

Now only the enchanted songless lark,
        the small one, the féerique
        flesh finer than beak,
hummer and fusser, darting untrapped spark,
        will rise at dawn
        as bird from lawn:
mistaken for a moth in citrus dark.

GENTLENESS OF FRIENDS

Gentleness of friends is the wine milder than milk
sipped in full summer under an open sky,
drained in sharp winter, cellared in catafalque:
honey of talk, healing, deep as a sigh.

Gentleness of friends is the cooling unguent juice
distilled from lips blistered with private grief:
ointment for ears which have heard the preposterous
    news
of self-disaster — deaf now beyond belief.

After that hour of pause when the shattered mind
craves but apartness, in the staunch gentles steal,
chalice-bearing like priests the milk stronger than
    wine —
honey of words, courtesy to calm and heal.

BAZAAR

No orientals with their laden trays,
their gorgeous burdened turbans, dusty smiles,
fast flying robes, sly slender dancing ways:
not here the colour and the heated drone
of singing salesmen. Never here the lean
and famished dogs, the blinded birds in song,
goblets or arak, spices, waxen fruit.
Now we are in the greylands of the north;
only the word bazaar sounds like a kiss
or a luxurious murmur. Neatly shod,
and dressed in disenchanting woollen coats
a pilgrim band perambulates the stalls;
the cake is weighed, its sugar towers touched,
the knitted gloves are tried, the vases wrapped.
Yet just a hint of recklessness and grace
caught from the skidding children, raises mirth
on kind deliberate faces, and translates
a cashy clink into gay castanets;
sound business men enjoy long unindulged
delight in trickery; wives bask in warmth
of buying goods which have no ready use;
though this is England, no disastrous frost
seeps through the gambler's pocket to his heart.

THE GREAT DAYS

Those were the great days, and the gracious days!
But did you say, my dear antagonist,
the past is all our treasure — that we live
now in the second-rate and the half-best?

Dear enemy, the times are always great
for the large-hearted. History is now,
and when we blame the meanness of our days
it may be we are meanly half alive
to their amazing import. True, the dwarfs
outnumber giants; it was always so;
all the more reason why we should not squeak
our pygmy voices in a petulance
at being small. The noble crimes, the guilt
hallowed by sacrifice, the strange crusades —
our idiom for describing them has changed;
but that they are is constant; and the Grail,
will-'o-the-wisp of goodness — we pursue
this in our several ways as did the knights,
undaunted that the hussifs and the shrews
outnumber Guinevere and brave Iseult.

Those were the great days! Yes, and these are great.
For who has his majority today
and rises to full stature, with the breath
of scientific dragons on his cheek,
he is as great as any hero born
in any century; greater perhaps:
having discarded cloth of gold and shield,
a faery faith and weapon mystical,
armoured in his frail envelope of flesh

and careless of transfiguring reward,
he stands within the nimbus of his times.
The light is strong because it pours from him:
the times are great when humans make them so.

CHRISTMAS BY THE SEASIDE

Terrible festival happiness of the cosy eaters
who have built a blinkered ark against the waters of
    war
and who, rising heavy from the table, draw curtains
    over their minds
lest brain should be keener and lighter than hearts
and stomachs are.

Unconsciously pitiful the artless limbs of the
    child,
moving frilly-encumbered round a festooned Christmas
    tree,
embryo woman form, potential of thoughtful beauty;
creature already cluttered with a tinsel destiny.

Outside in the black world beyond the snug harbour
the terrible killing continues, but inside the thin
    pity
has been so diminished by custom and rehearsal
it has become irritation at the radio voice from the
    city.

Surely, surely the anguish and the exquisite hope
of life that is stauncher than flesh and domestic
    emotion
are implicit in the surf and the spray and the
    disturbing stranger,
the skeleton at the feast, the ghost thrown up by
    the ocean?

ANDERSEN'S MERMAID
(a happy ending)

Nereid floats in the poetry of dreams,
rising above the rippled silver disc
of cerulean depth through which she swims
to gaze on earth and take a human risk.

Nemophilous the glad to which she floats,
monster and pigmy circled, and her eyes
endewed with fantasy divide the motes
of dancing leaves whose dappled panoplies

hide the one face, the face which is her good.
Vines and lianas tangle and impede
her shining devious progress to his wood:
at last it is by him that she is freed.

The Prince, attendant on his certain fate,
bemused by dream, yet comes awake in time —
seeks the sea's edge before it is too late
and with grave speech, in a most gracious mime

makes known his sure reciprocal accord.
And of such meeting simply need be said,
Nereid loves him, takes him for her lord,
and with most courteous passion are they wed.

Palm
and
Oak II*

1973

AUTHOR'S NOTE:

This collection contains poems from *In Circles*, *Palm and Oak (I)*, and *Contrasts* — published in Britain and the West Indies, and broadcast in various lands. "Poet's Cottage" is Wordsworth's home, Dove Cottage; and the Sad Pedant was De Quincey the opium eater. "While the Young Sleep" was an international prizewinner. Some of these poems were requested from Africa, Britain and France; they were written in various parts of the world and at various times of my life. They portray the tropical and Nordic strains in my ancestry, hence the title.

This edition is limited to 300 copies all numbered and signed by the author.

I dedicate it to daughters Phina and Sonia.

Editor's note*

Palm and Oak II contained poems from *In Circles, Palm and Oak*, and *Contrasts*, plus a handful of new poems. The new poems follow.
The reprinted poems were "Love for an Island", "Gentleness of Friends", "Poet's Cottage", "The Great Days", "The True-Born Villager", "While the Young Sleep", "Fugitive Hummingbird", "With Time a Threatened Currency", "Turn the Leaves", "Resistance", "The Perfection Seekers", "Maine", "Wind from the Park", "Now in our Times", "Expatriates", and "To London".

TRIO BY LAMPLIGHT

For David once upon a time

Hiawatha
Huckleberry
Fauntleroy...
Look long, for this may be the last year when within
    one taut brown skin
three story-book boys are tangled into one:
This is the hour when homework must be done.
The young Chief's fringe dips raven in the glow:
His slanting eyes of Brave or Eskimo
narrow above squared paper, bleak and white.
The nine-times table is a shocking fight;
his muscles ripple, he attacks the column
just like an Indian warrior stern and solemn.
"Arithmetic's not fair!" declares the boy's
precise, patrician voice (Lord Fauntleroy's);
appealing, throws a sidewise look of love
at Dad his helper; sidewise as we move
we see the profile proud, hear argument
in tones remote from wigwam or from tent,
his chubby, almost baby look diminished.
Then Huckleberry yells: "Shucks, Dad, I'm finished!
Gosh darn it, nine-times eight are seventy-two!"
jumps to his feet, crows cockadoodle do,
pushes his books away. "When do we eat?"
But pausing first within the slanting plane
of lamplight, he's the little Squire again:
"Dad, a boy took my kite. He said it was
a paper thing. I snatched it back, because
think of the time and labour kites require!"
He smiles with pride, the selfish little Squire.

And Hiawatha adds: "My kites are strong
as I've made bows and arrows for so long."
Then Huck leaps forward in a famished spate,
rushes into the kitchen, brings a plate
to stoke him up for mischief, and the three
inseparable boys eat sleepily
    at last; well-loved well-fed
tumbling in one brown body up to bed.

COMBATANTS ABROAD*

We who were born and breathed in open spaces,
And warm the blood of the restless in our veins,
Are now companion to those golden faces
Making their secret way through jungle lanes.

Back home, our people in their lamplit dark
Relaxing over newsprint, jerk and stand
Transfixed to learn that arrogant and loud
Havoc has lashed another hapless land.

That brown face lifted to the argent sky
To watch the birdlike swoop, with flowering mouth
Parted in wonder, spatters out to die
For things uncomprehended in his south.

Part-comprehending, we who move confined
By loyal duties to a modern state,
Face the same fate: creep with the brave and blind
Towards some goal as yet undesignated.

---

* This poem was rewritten for *Palm and Oak II* from an original entitled "Colonial
  Soldiers," written in London during the Second World War. The original version appears
  in the Appendix .

THE CHILD'S RETURN

For Jean Rhys

I remember a fair tall island
floating in cobalt paint
The thought of it is a childhood dream
torn by a midnight plaint

There are painted ships and rusty ships
that pass the island by,
and one dark day I'll board a boat
when I am ready to die

The timbers will creak and my heart will break
and the sailors will lay my bones
on the stiff rich grass, as sharp as spikes,
by the volcanic stones.

LONE CACTUS

Lone cactus, thinker
flowering in desert sands of war
uncrushed by the tanks of violence, springing green
against the burning sky and deadly battle:
You, oh my gentle,
my lover, speaking England
with your grave eyes and stubborn patient hands —
Oh I have seen you darken
with Abyssinian grief
and seen the rage in your eyes
lit by those fires of Spain
I have seen your flesh stripped
Like the torn flesh of India
and I have kissed on your mouth
the cries of Jews slain.
And so I know
that your apartness is but a waiting
your silence the crouch of strength
your thinking a hope in struggle
yourself the first and last warrior
Lone cactus thinker my gentle my England.

RETURN

Coming back to my house
from which I had been absent
so long, so long,
I found it ravaged of all
save you, my shrine and my song.
    Savage the winds rake:
yet the bamboo does not break.

O land which stood firm
through that shaking and horror,
O heart, O heart,
beating scornful and cool
through that tearing apart!
O land, O heart, O shrine —
strong, constant, and mine.

GHOSTS IN A PLANTATION HOUSE

Strangest of all strange things is the presence
   of strangers
In the rooms and the haunts and the glades of the
   dearly known.
Small wonder the slave girl moans and the French
   priest talks
And Victorian Doctors stroll out in the moonlight
   for walks.

Shallow in graves of loam in diminished acres —
Diminished by predator buyers assisted by drink —
Lie the skeletal forms of pets from an earlier
   period:
An occupation more gracious; a grace under God.

At last the young Laird awakens to his endowment.
"What's mine is mine!" he says. And to hell with
   you all.
Leave the place empty and leave it to the spirits
Until the day when my youngling son inherits.

But land is land and the predators are busy.
From an enchanted enclave of long days past
Nobody wants to move. Both ghosts and lawyers are
   waiting
Deep in the shadows: the struggle not yet abating.

Uncollected
Poems

TRANSFIGURATION[*]

Carrying precious weight,
The noble trees
Proud of their snowy freight
Solemnly freeze;
Under white branches flow
Cotton-wool streams,
Making this Buffalo
City of Dreams.

Buffalo, Bargain Sales,
Babbitts, and such
Turn into fairy-tales
At winter's touch.
They will grow drab again,
But will not know
Why there's a source of pain
In melting snow.

* "Transfiguration" is the earliest surviving poem by Phyllis Allfrey. It accompanied a
letter to Mrs Adele Emery (then Mrs John Oliphant), one of Allfrey's oldest and dearest
friends, dated October 21, 1932. It is included here with grateful acknowledgment to the
late Mrs Emery.

HYMN FOR 1940

Refujesus, weak but wild
Fugitive young English child,
Sitting on a stranger's knee
Ponder your lost family.

Fain we'd have you homeward bound —
Gracious God, and how! — but not
Till we've made this land a place
Where a child may show his face.

THE UNDERGROUND TIMES

Alone the mother grieves
for her lost children,
covered with robins' leaves
of silver dollars and dimes.
Such is the sky's commotion
and such the underground times,
that there is more than a flood,
more than a rampant ocean,
more than a river of blood
between her and her young:
between the safe limbs flung
douce on a distant bed
and the impertinent head
of one who gave flesh for breath —
vitality to cheat death.

These are the tides
which cut the mother off from her young children...
The white war faces of women streaming
                    along grey London streets;
Greedy Atlantic, teeming
with steel amphibious snare;
the hostile heavens, gleaming
with murder, from the air;
while far away a little boy lies dreaming —
drowned in his mother's hair.
The little girl lies still, her tranquil mind
unstained by sickly doubt or frightened yearning.
So soft they lie, so sleepy blind —
and yet —

the bricks around their home are burning.
To be a dweller in a bombarded hive
and to emerge alive
is no mean feat,
my sweet.
"The dily pipers call us nobl'-an-brive,
but cold is wot we are, and 'ungry too:
that goes for you an' you an' you an' you an' you.
Say, could you keep your seven children clean
sleeping in a disused latrine?
We got to spend our 'ard-earned cash on guns,
same as that 'Itler, see? No soap — no buns!"
The M.P. stalks
between the prostrate bodies. As he walks
he thinks of light and space and air and food.
Being a Red,
and from the Caucus viewpoint better dead,
he'd gladly share
with the disconsolate crowd space, food and air,
if he could have his hot bath in solitude.
But the people who walk in darkness see no light
    at all —
no light save the recurrent cruel moon,
aide-de-camp to enemy planes,
Grant us, O Lord, another day.

That grave young Doctor, thinking he can do
his best for man by examining a few
of the latest Shelter insect-bites,
but being too deep in love to study bugs
with ardour in decaying rugs,
pulls out his notebook and writes:

Tread lightly, love, beneath the falling bomb,
Walk graciously, my dear, beside the crater:
there is just time for beauty and aplomb —
and history is your adjudicator.

Your bearing in this hour so wanton-grim,
Your gesture and your voice, court no forgetting.
Tread proudly, love, and grasp the hand of he
Who stands unchanged by war's vain pirouetting.

      Above in the mist
      the gladiator boys
      release their killing noise.
      Their lips are brave and stern,
      their eyes are glassy-triste:
      but how they rejoice
      to see London burn!

Killing they know not when nor whom,
killing the infant in the womb,
killing the worker at his bench
and the non-political serving wench.

      Over another city
      some thousand miles away,
      our gladiator boys,
      likewise debunking pity
      drop tons of bombs per day.
      Oh what duplicity:
      Oh what Aryan Goys!
      Oh I say!

BEETHOVEN IN THE HIGHLANDS

Like conscript soldiers, her fingers march on the keys,
While an unrhythmic grief assaults her throat.
Out in the bay listless, irresolute seas
Whip the andante to a single note.

War of the heart, and battle out of reach!
Landscape of Argyll seen through pensive glass,
Will the machine-gun bullets litter this beach
And shrapnel scar the children on the grass?

The scherzo now; for it is yet too soon
To press the *Marche Funebre* or to bombard
The greyness of a Highland afternoon
With that crescendo pitiful and hard.

The great deaf German sings to deafened ears,
And darkened minds anticipate the shriek
Of anti-aircraft guns and loyal cheers.
Stop the offensive! Let adagio speak...

Those first grave chords, fluted and clarion, pierce
The bogus hatreds and the native pride.
Brothers in music, halting, deny their fierce
Sick passion for the Rhineland or the Clyde.

The great deaf German groped for this, and more.
Giving his brain and heart as food for sound;
He gave himself for the Argyllshire shore,
And gave himself for men the world around.

SEASIDE IN NOVEMBER

Now that the season is past, only those children stay
who were born with salty hair and sand in their toes;
the dogs that lollop along the waterfront
were littered in brine and nourished on herring-roes.

A ship in autumn distress draws to the bays
of friendly windows, with its imploring horn,
only those mothers who gazed on the tumbling sea
with the veiled captive eyes of the unborn.

The little streets are near-empty, the air is chill;
the passers-by are uncles and aunts and boys
on errand bicycles; the hotel-crushed hill
has shot its last false salvo of goodbye noise.

The town is no longer a boarding house: the beach
is a sweeping of frozen sugar dyed sunset-peach.

THE CHRISTMAS STROLLERS

'Tis Christmas eve, and cool. With quiet feet
The strolling singers cross to where the street
Splinters with silver, like a jagged street.

Imagine! In a land devoid of snow
The starlight makes a frosted festoon show,
Mock fir-trees lifting up their fruits aglow.

What does it signify? That everywhere,
From polar wastes to palmy hemisphere
The world keeps tryst with a remembrance clear.

And the remembrance... Just some common hay
Smoothed in a box against a Boy's birthday.
Yet see! The oxen curl their hoofs to pray.

O, what a childish fancy! That is why
All children love it so, and glorify
the tender legend which will never die.

And that is why, like children, strollers gaze
At neighbours' Christmas trees through starry haze
And to the Child their simple carols raise.

DOMINICA, LAST HAUNT OF THE CARIBS

Queen of the Caribbean! Solemn peaks
of jagged mountains pierce your misty sky,
Down the deep valleys rolling thunder speaks
The rain-clouds burst the torrent passes by.
And through the curtain like a bridal veil
The sun peeps forth and all the colours pale
Of soft-hued rainbow splendour, dimmed with tears,
Light up each scene as fairyland appears.

Green palms stand out with leaves like ancient lace,
Tall trees begemmed with raindrops take new grace,
As nature beautifies the beautiful. And then
In sheltered nooks appear the huts of men,
Then men themselves, last vestige of the race
That Dominica's mountains still embrace.

NATURE TOYS OF DOMINICA
Verses for Little Children

THE TREE BOAT

I run around the breezy land
holding out an eager hand,
and from red-bugged branches floats
a perfect fleet of little boats.

I seize the first one I can find —
its prow is sharp and well-designed
its outer hulk is painted dark:
inside is gold, like Noah's Ark.

I take my boat out for a sail
in pond or pool, bathtub or pail,
pleased as a joker with my toy —
Nature's free gift to a little boy.

THE TROPICAL BABY

While they are playing in the snows
And waving chubby, frozen hands,
My little darling digs her toes
Into the warm West Indian sands;

They wear woollens, she goes bare;
They have shovels, she has a spade.
Their laughter strikes the frosty air
While hers spins out from sun to shade.

"Mother!" they cry. She neither knows
What mother means, nor does she care.
She sits and contemplates her toes
Thinking they must be playthings rare.
There is a smile about her mouth
Of infant jocularity;
She is a cherub of the south,
A little mermaid from the sea.

THE PALM HORSE

O who would want to buy a horse
Or even make one out of wood,
When the palm-tree drops a horse
Fifty times as good?

He has a great long bushy tail
And a lovely leathery head;
After I've ridden him for miles
He falls asleep tied to my bed.

THE PAWPAW FLUTE

Learn of my lips, little pawpaw flute,
    gaily, greedily,
The song of the wonderful melon fruit
    on the pawpaw street.

    Like the palm-leaf steed
    and the boat-tree boat,

this hollow reed
sings a lovely note

of a land that teems
with fabulous plants,
to match the long dreams
of what every child wants.

THE LA BELLE
(Flying beetle with Headlamps)

I see his bright green headlamps go ahead
as I lie in the soft darkness of my bed;
he is a flying car all polished brown,
and on my little desk he touches down.

He travels up the straight boards of the floor,
pausing to make a swinging left detour.
Now and again he switches off, and I
imagine he is charging up to fly.

The beams of his great emerald lamps allume
the ceiling, walls and corners of my room.
Who would not wish to own a car that flies,
a flying beetle car with magic eyes?

Rose O*

---

* As editor of the *Dominica Herald* and later *The Star* newspaper, Allfrey published a large number of satirical rhymes, most often with political themes, under the pen name of Rose O (a play on Roseau, the capital of Dominica). Some representative examples of these are reprinted here.

MY NATIONAL SONG

Oh they've had it too sweet too long
Is the theme of my national song.
   One hour in the sun for a fish
   will spoil the tastiest dish,
   while a day in an open tin
   will harden the bread from the bin;
   when it comes to political man
   ten years is an awful long span,
   and for most politicians alive
   the maximum term should be five.

   Does power corrupt and rot?
   Yes, if you misuse it a lot.
   Does too much cash undermine
   the men with the party line?
   Of course it does, if they grip
   the line till they sink the ship.
   The solution is up to you:
   sack the captain and change the crew,
   for they've had it too sweet too long.
   That's the theme of my national song.

THE ROADS

And do the roads wind uphill all the way?
   — Yes, to the very end.
But if they need more finance, who will pay?
   — England, my friend.

What if the landslides gush and waters roar?
   — Nature's to blame.
And at P.W.D. who keeps the score?
   — I name no name!

Shall I sell out and buy a Roseau lot,
   — Near voting day.
Since there's no road to my banana plot?
   — I cannot say.

How many votes are there to half-a-mile?
   — That would depend
On peasant sense and smart speech making style.
   — Just guess, my friend.

TALKERS
Nonsense Rhyme

Mutter mutter bread and butter.
First a Talker with a stutter:
Next, far worse than any stammer
Comes a Second with no grammar.

Better, better, bet — 'tis bettered:
Here's a Talker not unlettered;
Someone used to Court proceedings,
Family and other pleadings.

If the Talker's uncommitted,
Reasonably nimble-witted
And objective...no objection.
If he's not...complete dejection.

ELECTORAL RHYME

Apres Bondié c'est La Ter,*
said the boy to his mater.
Apres sisserou c'est crapaud,
said the cow to the buffalo.
Apres Bondié c'est La Ter,
said the boy's gloomy pater.
But he paused for a drink
and fell over the brink,
to the depth of the crater.
It is later than you think.

---

* *After God it is the Land* is the motto emblazoned on the Dominica crest.

DE DONKEY DERBY

O de Labour Party has changed it style:
Is donkeys not horses runnin de mile
If you want to see Labour Society
You should ha attended de Donkey Derby.

I glad de tickets collect and pay
Before de rain fall to spoil de day.
So de VIPS in deir fancy close
Could go an put money on de donkey nose.

Is to help de poor in de Hospital
Dat de Donkey Derby get run at all,
An de country people come dere in bus
Shoutin for de winner like de res of us.

But de ting I went dere myself to see
Is de Labour Party in Society:
I very sorry for de poor cole people
Who had to shelter near Ma James' Home steeple.

But one little pusson don follow de crowd
An she stay in she house when she see big cloud
(Since dey push her out of deir society):
Is dat one-time politician Madame Porte LaPluie.

UWI DIALOGUE*

— Say, who is the little old lady
that gave in her resignation?
— Well, she's only a Royal Auntie,
no need to create a sensation.

— But didn't she raise plenty money
for the UWI Foundation
in the hope we would all be students
of a great West Indies Nation?

— Man, the times are now too trendy
to be bothering with Aunt Alice.
So forget that we owe her anything;
she can get her reward at the Palace.

— But I love the Royal Auntie
and I hate your talking so callous.
I prefer the Royal Ex-Chancellor
to Professors of Hate and Malice.

— And who is that little short doctor
who says we must have A-levels?
— Oh he's only Doc Eric Williams,
in his youth he was quite a devil.

— Remember his famous hist'ry book
To San Fernando from Seville?
Now he's only an Uncle Tom character
in a great big carnival revel.

---

* The acronym UWI stands for the University of the West Indies.

— And what kind of character are you?
— I'm a gem of O-level power.
I see a Nation in a grain of sand.
An eternity in a dark flower.

I want to change UWI
before the clock strikes another hour.
And Aunties and Uncles will have no place
in my campus' ebony tower.

SUGARDY-CANDY

All is sugardy-candy in the Chamber
For the Guvment and the merchants are as one.
They have set aside their feud
For the trade and general good.
Oh what a lovely island in the sun.

All is sugardy-candy with bananas,
For the growers and the Guvment make the Board.
There's no hardship in a cess
Till the prices get less and less,
And the peasant finds out what he can't afford.

All is sugardy-candy in the nation
(Or should I say "Associated State"?)
Simply ask the little man
How he views the five-year plan,
And he'll silently hold out an empty plate.

All was sugardy-candy in Assembly
Until Eugenia came upon the scene.
But she brought a squeeze of lime
Through her connaissance of crime.
Now the sugardy-candy swizzle's turning green.

THE HUNTING OF THE SMIDER-SNARK
(with acknowledgments to Lewis Carroll)

Note: The word "Smider" is an abbreviation of Small Islander.

"Just the place for a Smider!" the Sergeant cried,
As he ambushed the Entrant with care,
Adjuring his men to remain at his side
In the heat of the afternoon glare.

"It's the Smiders cause trouble!" He said it twice.
"That alone should encourage the Force."
"It's the Smiders cause trouble!" He said it thrice;
And the newspapers print it, of course.

The trap was complete: it included a Sport,
And an expert in small island foods;
A Barrister, brought to arrange the deport,
And a Bailiff to value the goods.

The Smider was famed for the number of things
He forgot when he boarded the ship:
His umbrella, his passport, his cutlass and rings,
And the clothes he had bought for his trip.

Some witnesses proved without error of law
That the hut was deserted when found,
But the Smider was caught with a noose in the raw
And put in the Immigrants' Pound.

Is it Belmont, Cascade, Cocorite or John-John?
"No matter — we'll winkle them out!"
Called the Valiant Inspector — and he thereupon
Banged the doors with his fists and did shout:

"You Grenadian! Kittitian! St Lucian! Hello!
Step out, you illegal P.I.!
Dominican, Vincentian — you Smiders, please show —
We're deporting you, see? Don't be shy!"

He had a large map representing the sea,
With just a few hillocks of land,
And the Smiders were sad when they found it to be
A hint they could well understand.

T'was pathetic, no doubt, when the Smiders found out
That the unit they thought of as swell
Had only one notion — to give them the ocean
And a bad reputation as well.

"Friends, Smiders and Countrymen, lend me your ears!"
(The Inspector was fond of quotations):
"Let us drink to your health, and you give me three
    cheers
While awaiting your quick deportations."

Said a Smider: "I've stayed in this land many years,
And the last weeks I spent in the prison;
My poor Smider mother will perish in tears
At the heartless *commesse** now arisen."

Sergeant said, "We shall all be most grieved, I
    believe
If you never set foot here again;
But surely, my man, when your mother took leave
She could have foreseen it all then?"

"Play the man!" cried Inspector in wrath as he saw
The Smider beginning to sob;

He remembered his brother in English Wishaw
(A stowaway migrant with job).

Yelled the Captain and Crew as the schooner hove to
(For Smiders are sailors of boats):
"Look out, loving friends, and take care what you do.
We Smiders have Federal votes!"

* *Commesse.* Smider patois for *confusion.* (Allfrey's note)

Appendix

COLONIAL SOLDIERS

We who were born and breathed in open spaces,
Who warm the blood of the restless in our veins,
Are now companion to those shut-in faces
Making their cautious way through narrow lanes.

Sometimes, arrested in the graying crowd
To study careful newsprint, see us stand
Transfixed to learn that arrogant and loud
Evil has dropped upon our guiltless land.

That brown face lifted to the argent sky
To watch the birdlike swoop, with flowering mouth
Parted in wonder, spatters out to die
For things uncomprehended in his south.

Uncomprehending, too, we move confined
By the strict gestures of the modern state,
And bearing arms march with the willing blind
Towards some goal as yet undesignate.

Lightning Source UK Ltd.
Milton Keynes UK
UKHW021301180822
407496UK00019B/359

9 780957 118751